MEXICO

Yu

Mexicali

El Centro

Brawley

8

Tijuana

C

San Diego

15

Santa Ana

Anaheim

Long Beach

HOLLYWOOD

Los Angeles

San Bernardino

Hesperia

Santa Clarita

Palmdale

Lancaster

Barstow

Mojave

Ridgecrest

40

Joshua Tree National Park

JOSHUA TREE NAT'L PARK

Colorado

Sea

River

Colorado

15

Las Vegas

Lake Mead

Meadow

Amargosa (intermittent)

DEATH VALLEY NATIONAL PARK

Los Angeles Aqueduct

▲ Mt. Whitney 14,495 ft.

KINGS CANYON NATIONAL PARK

SEQUOIA NAT'L PARK

Kings

San Joaquin

Clovis

Fresno

Los Banos

erced

Bakersfield

Wasco

Porterville

Visalia

5

California Aqueduct

Avenal

Atascadero

Santa Maria

Santa Barbara

Ventura

Santa Barbara Channel

CHANNEL ISLANDS NAT'L PARK

Salinas

Salinas

Big Sur

Monterey

Monterey Bay

Santa Cruz

San Jose

o

Alcatraz

PACIFIC OCEAN

N

Distance in miles

0   20   40   60   80

CAROL M. HIGHSMITH AND TED LANDPHAIR

CALIFORNIA

A PHOTOGRAPHIC TOUR

CRESCENT BOOKS

NEW YORK

FRONT COVER: The "Lone Cypress," one of the distinctively windblown Monterey varieties of the evergreen found on the shoreline of the famous 17-Mile Drive on the Monterey Peninsula. It is said to be the most photographed tree in the world. (Permission for use granted by the Pebble Beach Company. All rights reserved.) BACK COVER: The pyramidal Transamerica Building has become a symbol of burgeoning San Francisco's Montgomery Street—the "Wall Street of the West." PAGE 1: The exclusive Art Deco Beverly Hills Hotel evokes the halcyon days of Hollywood. Its "in crowd" made sure to be seen there. PAGES 2–3: The 1932 Bixby Creek Bridge, on breathtaking Route 1 between Monterey and Big Sur, was an engineering marvel.

This 1999 edition is published by Crescent Books®,
an imprint of
Random House Value Publishing, Inc.,
280 Park Avenue, New York, N.Y. 10017.

Crescent Books and colophon
are registered trademarks of
Random House Value Publishing, Inc.

Random House
New York • Toronto • London • Sydney • Auckland
http://www.randomhouse.com/

Printed and bound in China

Library of Congress Cataloging-in-Publication Data

Highsmith, Carol M.
California / Carol M. Highsmith and Ted Landphair.
p. cm. — (A photographic tour)
Includes index.
ISBN 0-517-20399-5 (hc: alk. paper)
1. California—Tours. 2. California—Pictorial works.
I. Landphair, Ted, 1942– . II. Title. III. Series:
Highsmith, Carol M., 1946– Photographic tour.
F859.3.H54 1999   98–31235
917.9404′53—dc21   CIP

8 7 6 5 4

Project Editor: Donna Lee Lurker
Production Supervisor: Milton Wackerow
Designed by Robert L. Wiser, Archetype Press, Inc.,
Washington, D.C.

All photographs by Carol M. Highsmith
unless otherwise credited: map by XNR Productions,
page 5; painting by Jeannette Maxfield Lewis, Monterey
Museum of Art collection, gift of Dr. and Mrs. James
Meier, page 6; Bison Archives, Hollywood, page 8; Regal
Biltmore Hotel, Los Angeles, page 9; Hotel Del
Coronado, Coronado, page 10; El Centro Chamber of
Commerce & Visitors Bureau, page 11; Calaveras
County Historical Society, courtesy of Robert Bach, page
12; Diamond Walnut Growers Inc., page 13; C.W.
Vernon, courtesy of Mayfield House B&B, Tahoe City,
page 14; Shasta Historical Society, page 15; Norton
Steenfott, courtesy of Kathleen Gordon-Burke, Eureka,
page 16; Rebecca Yerger, Napa, page 17; Prints and
Photographs Division, Library of Congress, page 18; San
Francisco Public Library, page 19; Hearst San Simeon
State Historical Monument, pages 20–21.

THE AUTHORS WISH TO THANK THE FOLLOWING FOR
THEIR GENEROUS ASSISTANCE AND HOSPITALITY IN
CONNECTION WITH THE COMPLETION OF THIS BOOK

Blue Violet Mansion, Napa;
Kathy and Bob Morris, proprietors

Cambria Pines Lodge, Cambria

Carter House Country Inn, Eureka

The Cannery Waterfront Restaurant,
Newport Beach

Centrella Inn, Pacific Grove;
Gary Luce, general manager

Gosby House Inn, Pacific Grove;
Tess Arthur, manager

Furnace Creek Inn, Death Valley;
Toni Jepson, manager

Heritage Park B&B Inn, San Diego;
Nancy Helspar, proprietor

Holiday Inn, Barstow

Idle Spurs Steakhouse, Barstow

Mayfield House B&B, Tahoe City;
Bruce and Cynthia Knauss, proprietors

O'Brien Mountain Inn, O'Brien;
Teresa and Greg Ramsey, proprietors

Piccadilly Inn, Fresno

Ramada Inn, El Centro

Sheraton Los Angeles International Airport,
Los Angeles

Westin South Coast Plaza, Costa Mesa

Jan Austerman, Napa Valley
Conference & Visitors Bureau

Mary Cochran, California Division of Tourism

Bill Gates, El Centro

Jennifer A. Gonzales, Anaheim/Orange County Visitor
& Convention Bureau

Kathleen Gordon-Burke, Eureka-Humboldt County
Convention & Visitors Bureau

Amy Herzog, Monterey Peninsula
Visitors & Convention Bureau

Cathy Kennerson, El Centro
Chamber of Commerce & Visitors Bureau

Stacey Litz, Los Angeles
Convention & Visitors Bureau

Louisa Miller, Barstow Area
Chamber of Commerce

Sarah Moore, San Luis Obispo County
Visitors & Convention Bureau

Jon Mozenter, Hollywood

Sandy Robinson, La Mesa

Bonnie Sharp, Redding
Convention & Visitors Bureau

Al and Janette Smith, Fresno

Joe Timko, San Diego
Convention & Visitors Bureau

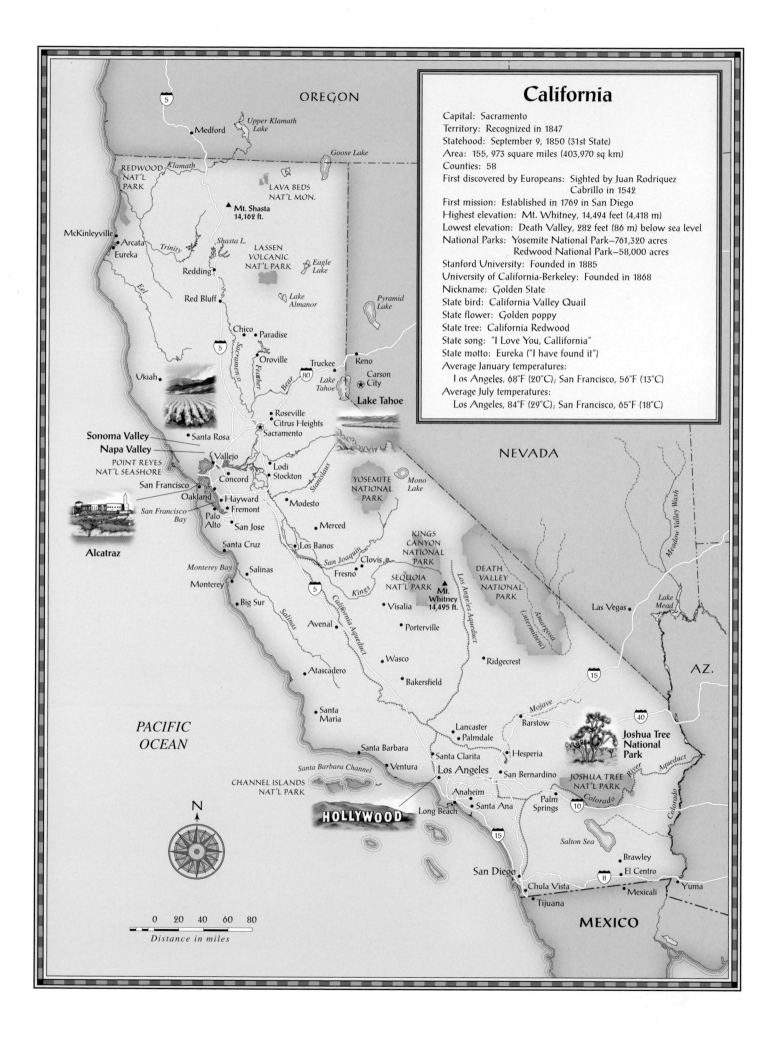

OREGON

⑤ Medford

Upper Klamath Lake

Goose Lake

REDWOOD NAT'L PARK

Klamath

LAVA BEDS NAT'L MON.

▲ Mt. Shasta 14,162 ft.

McKinleyville • Arcata
Eureka •

Trinity

Shasta L.

LASSEN VOLCANIC NAT'L PARK

Eagle Lake

Eel

Redding •

Red Bluff •

Lake Almanor

Pyramid Lake

Chico •
• Paradise

⑤ • Oroville

Sacramento
Feather

Truckee • • Reno

Carson City ★

Lake Tahoe

Ukiah •

Bear
⑧⓪

Lake Tahoe

Roseville
Citrus Heights ★ Sacramento

Sonoma Valley
Napa Valley

POINT REYES NAT'L SEASHORE

• Santa Rosa

Vallejo •

Concord •

• Lodi
• Stockton

Stanislaus

NEVADA

San Francisco •
Oakland •
• Hayward
San Francisco Bay
Palo Alto •
• Fremont
• San Jose

Alcatraz

• Modesto

• Merced

YOSEMITE NATIONAL PARK

Mono Lake

Meadow Valley Wash

Santa Cruz •

Monterey Bay

• Los Banos

San Joaquin

• Clovis
Fresno •

KINGS CANYON NATIONAL PARK

DEATH VALLEY NATIONAL PARK

• Salinas

SEQUOIA NAT'L PARK

▲ Mt. Whitney 14,495 ft.

Los Angeles Aqueduct

Amargosa (intermittent)

Monterey •

Kings

• Visalia

Big Sur •

Salinas

Avenal •

• Porterville

• Las Vegas

Lake Mead

California Aqueduct

Atascadero •

• Wasco

• Bakersfield

• Ridgecrest

PACIFIC OCEAN

• Santa Maria

• Lancaster
• Palmdale

Mojave
• Barstow

AZ.

⑮

Joshua Tree National Park

Santa Barbara •

• Santa Clarita

• Hesperia

④⓪

Santa Barbara Channel

• Ventura

Los Angeles •

• San Bernardino

JOSHUA TREE NAT'L PARK

CHANNEL ISLANDS NAT'L PARK

Anaheim •
• Santa Ana

Palm Springs •

Colorado River

Aqueduct

N

HOLLYWOOD • Long Beach

⑩

Colorado

Salton Sea

Colorado

• Brawley

0 20 40 60 80

San Diego •

Chula Vista •

⑧ • El Centro

Mexicali •

Yuma •

Distance in miles

Tijuana •

MEXICO

M ANY AMERICANS THINK THEY KNOW CALIFORNIA. But the Golden State never ceases to amaze even Californians themselves. A simple description seems like a contradiction: it's warmer and colder, higher and lower, more rural and urban, more heavily populated and sparsely populated than many people realize. It is also bigger, drier, more forested, agricultural, ethnically diverse, historic, and beautiful, too. The state's seemingly paradoxical nature stems, in part, from the fact that it is a long way—in miles, culture, and lifestyle—between San Diego and the Oregon line.

Rambunctious California defines the New West, but it retains countless elements of the Old West as well. It is conservative in places, liberal in others. California boasts the "genuine article" Westerners: cowboys, lumberjacks, roustabouts, and miners. But it also has its share of what the Center for the New West calls "cow-free watering holes for weekend cowboys and coastal yuppies looking for a shake-and-bake wilderness experience." And politicians who hold statewide office must somehow meld the interests of ranchers, fishermen, farm workers, filmmakers, business executives, environmentalists, the "Jeep Cherokee crowd" of suburbanites, and myriad other constituencies.

California is still a state of immigrants. Not just the highly publicized newcomers from Asia, Mexico, and other Latin American countries, but also a continuing influx of new arrivals looking to "reinvent" themselves or their lives. To a never-ending stream of settlers, mild as well as wild California offers what *Time* in 1993 called "liberation and excitement . . . as the ultimate, myth-making destination, tantalizing the daydreams of restless souls itching to pick up and move."

California's 155,973 square miles encompass incredibly varied terrain. More than fifty peaks in the long Sierra Nevada Mountains top five thousand feet, including Mount Whitney at 14,495 feet—the highest in the continental states. The blistering Badwater salt flats in Death Valley lie 282 feet below sea level, and the *bottom* of the Salton Sea near Palm Springs is far lower than that. And besides the San Andreas Fault—the world's longest fracture—there are other cataclysmic geological battle lines along the earth's tectonic plates that lie in California or just off its coastline. There are also dormant volcanoes in Owens Valley where its great mountain passes are now adorned with turbines (to harness the ever-blowing wind of the California Southland) and a lush interior basin that is drained by the occasionally raging Sacramento and San Joaquin Rivers.

Except in the mountains and the far-northern redwood and sequoia forests, fall and spring are fleeting events, if they are noticeable at all. In much of the state the climate ranges from a brief, moderate, sometimes rainy winter to a long, dry, and pleasant summer. (Death Valley summers are not temperate, of course; in the nation's hottest place the *mean* July temperature is 102 degrees Fahrenheit.) It was the state's golden sunshine—which *Life* once called "the most valuable ingredient of the California way of life"—as well as the famous gold rush of the middle of the nineteenth century that gave the state its nickname. And the state's affinity for gold does not end there. The golden poppy is the state flower, and there is even the South Fork golden trout, the state fish. The name "California"—"abounding in gold"—first appeared as a mythical island east of Eden in a sixteenth-century Spanish romance novel. The name was at first applied to Lower (*Baja*) California and later extended to all of Spain's new holdings along the western Pacific Rim.

Jeannette Maxfield Lewis, who owned a home in Pebble Beach and painted many scenes of Big Sur, Monterey, and Carmel, completed On the Carmel Coast *in about 1935. It depicts the rocky shoreline that draws visitors to the area's dramatic 17-Mile Drive. The painting is part of the collection of the Monterey Museum of Art.*

The careers of Clark Gable and Jean Harlow were in full bloom when they made Wife Vs. Secretary *at the MGM Studios in 1936. Harlow, age twenty-five, would be dead of encephalatis a year later.*

Like other western states, California is a series of what Phillip M. Burgess and Richard F. O'Donnell of the Center for the New West call "urban archipelagos and large city-states surrounded by vast empty quarters." Paradoxically, California is the nation's most populated, and urban, state, yet 45 percent of its land mass is owned by the federal government. America's biggest county (San Bernardino) and the world's most sprawling city (Los Angeles, at 467 square miles, often lampooned as "a hundred suburbs in search of a city") are both in California.

California's ethnic mosaic began in 1770, the moment Catholic missionaries traveled north from Spain's Mexican colony and built missions in an effort to convert the mostly passive Native American tribes. In 1812, Russians established a foothold at Fort Ross, north of present-day San Francisco, but they were mostly interested in hunting sea otters, not putting down roots; when the otter supply was all but exterminated, they left the area. The river that empties into the Pacific near their settlement was, however, named the Russian River in their wake. Mexicans continued to filter north into present-day California after their nation gained independence from Spain in 1822. Americans of many heritages broke down the doors to California in their frantic search for gold following its discovery at Sutter's Mill in 1848. Asian migration began with the fifteen thousand Chinese laborers brought in to work in the mines and on the railroad soon after statehood in 1850. Italian and Portuguese fishermen and their families started small colonies along the coast. In 1960, non-Hispanic whites accounted for 80 percent of California's population. Four decades later, that figure has dropped to 55 percent. One in five Californians is Hispanic, and the Asian population is approaching 10 percent.

Although the world's first "automobile migration" began into California as early as the 1920s, the most disruptive relocation on wheels occurred during the Great Depression in the

late 1930s. Its misery was compounded by a lingering drought that had turned America's Great Plains into an unbearable Dust Bowl. Hundreds of thousands of farm families loaded their possessions onto trucks and struck out for California's "land of milk and honey." During this period, proposed reforms to help the threadbare "Okies," like Upton Sinclair's EPIC ("end poverty in California") Program, were met with sometimes virulent opposition.

It was the decades of the 1940s through the 1970s that California's population truly erupted. Everything new and improved seemed to start there: big-budget motion pictures, modern weapons design and production, transcontinental television, the personal-computer revolution, and even "surfer" music that extolled carefree "California dreamin'." For what seem to be dozens of reasons about which few can agree, California has also become a magnet for individualists, nonconformists, and eccentrics. Cults and fringe religions—fewer today than decades ago—seem to sprout like mushrooms in a rain forest. Beatniks, "flower children," and "I amists" are just three of the more benign groups. "Peaceniks" and runaways hieing to San Francisco were reminded to "be sure to wear some flowers in your hair." Neal Peirce and Jerry Hagstrom, in their *Book of America*, called California of the 1970s "an unstratified society made up of communities of strangers." As Walter Duranty said in the 1940s, "Iowa gets here and goes crazy."

California politics has been marked by a passion for ballot initiatives and referenda—including Proposition 13, the largest property-tax-cut measure in history, in 1978—and a parade of colorful leaders of every stripe. What other state could produce, in fairly short order, three more dissimilar governors than the avuncular Earl Warren, a future United States chief justice; genial president-to-be Ronald Reagan; and distracted "Governor Moonbeam" Jerry Brown? Assembly speakers have included "Boss" Jess Unruh, who coined the maxim, "Money is the

At the Biltmore Hotel's extravagant opening gala in Los Angeles in 1923, three thousand guests dined in eight rooms decorated with a profusion of California flowers to the accompaniment of seven orchestras and singing canaries.

9

The Hotel Del Coronado opened in 1888 as a grand Victorian seaside resort on an island across San Diego Bay. Ever since, the "Del" has been a favorite celebrity haunt and movie locale.

mother's milk of politics," and effervescent Willie Brown, the state's most radiant African-American political success story, who would later return to his hometown of San Francisco and win the mayor's job. And among U.S. senators: former soft-shoe man George Murphy; classic liberal and world-class runner Alan Cranston; no-nonsense former college president S.I. Hayakawa; and, beginning in 1993, an unprecedented two women in the same delegation—former San Francisco mayor Dianne Feinstein and onetime stockbroker Barbara Boxer. Not to be overlooked in the panoply of unpredictable California politicians are onetime Carmel mayor Clint Eastwood, pop-star turned congressman Sonny Bono, and of course Richard M. Nixon, an obscure U.S. representative until he was tapped as Dwight D. Eisenhower's running mate. Nixon lost a bitter campaign for California governor, then won two presidential elections before resigning his office in the disgrace of Watergate in 1974.

All of this is relatively recent history, as, in fact, is much of the California story. Spanish explorers advanced as far as the lower Colorado River as early as 1540 but never bothered to cross into the barren desert before them. It was left to Spanish seafarers Juan Rodríguez Cabrillo and Bartolomé Ferrelo to sail the California coastline, Cabrillo landing first in San Diego Bay in 1542. On his 'round-the-world adventure, Sir Francis Drake, the British captain, stopped at San Francisco Bay long enough to repair his ships in 1579; he even claimed the territory for his homeland, christening it "Nova Albion" (New England). But he did not stick around long enough to secure the claim. And Spanish galleons called at San Diego for provisioning on their long trans-Pacific journeys to and from Manila. But it was left to Catholic missionaries to spur settlement of California along *El Camino Real* (the Royal Highway), a crude trail from San Diego past San Francisco to Sonoma. Twenty-one missions—and the *pueblos* (towns), *presidios* (forts), orchards, and cattle ranches that sprang up around them—dotted the highway about a day's journey apart. Along U.S. Highway 101 today, a few symbolic examples of the old mission bells, painted green, can still be found. The missions drastically declined in influence under Mexican rule. The government secularized them and sold off most of their land.

Many early-nineteenth-century settlers, including Swiss John A. Sutter, on whose land gold would be discovered in 1848, entered California via a spur of the Santa Fe Trail. Sutter got a huge land grant that included the site of present-day Sacramento. He built a fort and served as an official Mexican representative in the region. Americans under Captain John C. Frémont, who was meandering through the West, ostensibly on a surveying mission, marched menacingly through Northern California. They seized the Sonoma *presidio* in 1846 and raised a flag emblazoned with the likeness of a grizzly bear. A version of the bear—now extinct in California—still hulks on the state flag. ("Yosemite" means grizzly bear in the original Native American language of the High Sierras.) The California Republic lasted less than a month. As the United States was invading Texas in an expansionist war with Mexico, American commander John D. Sloat was raising the Stars and Stripes in California at the old Spanish provincial capital of Monterey. As John Gunther would write in the 1940s, "the westward swell of migration was bound to reach the Pacific; the United States without California would have been as ridiculous as France without Brittany or England without Kent; politically, geographically, humanly, the impulse to fill the great bowl of the West was unavoidable and irresistible."

Defeated Mexico formally ceded the territory to the United States in the Treaty of Guadalupe Hidalgo in 1848, and California's first constitution was framed by a convention meeting under a U.S. military governor in Monterey the following year. Weary of Indian and bandit raids in the turbulent months after the defeat of Mexico, Californians not only quickly ratified the constitution, they also elected and inaugurated a state governor and legislature—even before Congress, in 1850, got around to making California the thirty-first state.

Two years earlier one of John Sutter's hands, James Marshall, found gold along the banks of the American River on Sutter's property northeast of Sacramento. Legend notwithstanding, it was not Marshall who shouted, "Eureka! I have found it!" Archimedes said it twenty-one centuries earlier during another sort of gold discovery. He had perfected a method to test the mineral's purity. "Eureka!" is, however, the complete official California state motto today.

Within a year of the discovery of gold, ten thousand prospectors had descended on the highlands, grabbing grubstakes irrespective of Sutter's claims, and turned the mountainous wilderness into the boomtown of Coloma. Soldiers deserted their companies and sailors their ships in the frenzy to find gold; one account found five hundred abandoned ships in San Francisco harbor at the height of the gold rush. In 1850, women were found to make up only 8 percent of the new state's population. More "Forty-niners" streamed into California by land across the searing desert; by portage over the Panama isthmus and thence by packet steamer up the Mexican and California coasts; and the long way, by sailing around Cape Horn. In the four years from 1848 to 1852, California's population increased seventeen-fold to two hundred fifty thousand. Much of the gold left California and helped to finance the nation's rise to superpower status. Overnight, San Francisco, which outfitted the gold rush, mushroomed from a

It was soon after Colorado River water was first delivered to the Imperial Valley through the Alamo Canal that El Centro sprang from the desert as an oasis of commerce and culture.

sleepy fishing port of one thousand people to a Queen City of fifty thousand—rich, raucous, and refined all at once. Libraries, opera houses, and newspapers sprang up, and writers like Mark Twain and Bret Harte glamorized the gold rush for a voracious audience back East.

The gold rush would be followed by lesser California "fevers"—in oil, citrus, vineyards, airplane manufacturing, high technology, and the making of movies—marked by great risk, adventure, and entrepreneurship. So successful did the California fishing industry become that the commercial fish catch, especially of tuna and sardines, topped one *billion* pounds in 1949. The catch, and business at canneries all along the coast, then declined precipitously, however, due to overfishing and the mysterious—though temporary—disappearance of sardines in the eastern Pacific.

Land and population booms far outpaced busts over the next century. One was triggered by the building of the transcontinental railroad, heading east out of Sacramento, during and immediately after the Civil War. The western leg, which met the eastern tracks at Promontory Point in Utah on May 12, 1869, was financed by the Central Pacific's "Big Four" millionaire financiers: Charles Crocker, Collis Huntington, Mark Hopkins, and Leland Stanford. They and others whom muckraking newspapers excoriated as "robber barons" built fancy mansions on San Francisco's Nob Hill.

Chief among the "yellow journalists"—a term that derived from the "Yellow Kid" comic strip and the yellow hue of the sensational "extra" broadsheets hawked on the street—was William Randolph Hearst, publisher of the *San Francisco Examiner*, who built a nationwide newspaper, magazine, and silent-movie empire. In 1919, upon the death of his mother, Hearst inherited rugged mountain property overlooking the ocean at San Simeon, midway down the

Mark Twain's yarn "The Celebrated Jumping Frog of Calaveras County," set in Angels Camp, was twenty-five years old when these Angels Camp students posed in front of the Altaville one-room school.

Pacific Coast. Over thirty years in collaboration with Paris-trained architect Julia Morgan, Hearst designed and built a lavish mountaintop mansion. It became the nation's most elaborate Shangri-La. Hearst installed his mistress, Marion Davies, and lavishly entertained Hollywood stars at the estate's glittering Casa Grande, enormous Roman and Neptune pools, sumptuous gardens, and mansion-sized guest houses.

Hearst Castle was built of heavy masonry in recognition of the area's vulnerability to earthquakes. Hearst knew well the ravages of the 1906 San Francisco quake that virtually destroyed the eastern half of the city and killed as many as one thousand people. Two more devastating quakes would strike the state: the Los Angeles temblor of 1971, centered in the crowded San Fernando Valley, sixty-four people died, whole sections of freeway collapsed, and more than $500 million in damage ensued; and the catastrophic Loma Prieta earthquake of 1989 flattened part of the San Francisco-Oakland Bay Bridge, ravaged the East Bay, darkened San Francisco for days, and triggered gas-line fires that consumed much of the city's Marina District. Remarkably, only one person died in the '89 quake.

California's abundant agricultural crops include walnuts distributed internationally by the Diamond Walnut Growers cooperative. Early equipment for sorting and sizing the nuts was crude but effective.

World War II brought another boom as hundreds of thousands of military personnel and defense workers, and their families, streamed into the state. California gained 1.5 million people during the war—San Diego grew by more than 150,000, a 78-percent jump. After the war, many of these newcomers stayed, fueling burgeoning markets in tract homes, strip shopping malls, automobiles, and appliances and other consumer goods. Fifth in state population in 1940, California jumped to second in the census a decade later, leapfrogging Pennsylvania, Ohio, and Illinois.

While California is sometimes pictured as a spaghetti bowl of freeways, fewer than six thousand miles of freeway were constructed after the first, from downtown Los Angeles to Pasadena, was finished in 1940. Other roads, such as several stretches of U.S. 101 not far from the Pacific Coast, were widened and given limited access like expressways, however.

Irrigation helped create an aromatic floral and citrus potpourri in California. Two seedless orange trees imported from Brazil in the 1890s presaged a giant industry of millions of orange, lemon, and grapefruit trees, and, at least until spreading suburban subdivisions overwhelmed many orchards, California rivaled Florida as a citrus producer. California also became the nation's leading supplier of almonds, walnuts, prunes, apricots, olives, avocados, and raisins. Vast rows of annual flowers drape parts of the landscape as well; they are cultivated for their seeds, which are packaged and sold worldwide. California wildflowers are unharvested, but they are a visual delight. Naturalist John Muir, explorer of the Yosemite Valley and co-founder of the Sierra Club, wrote of the Sonora highlands, "For a distance of 400 miles, your foot crushed a hundred flowers at every step."

California is also among the nation's top three states in the production of oil, timber, dairy products, ocean fish, and sixty or more minerals. More than 90 percent of the world's borates, used in everything from soap to fiberglass, for instance, come from California. Two generations of Americans learned about "borax"—the lay term for borates—first on radio and then on television, from the "Old Ranger," played on TV by Ronald Reagan, during stories of the California desert on "Death Valley Days."

California's 1,254-mile coastline is as varied as the state itself. In the south, the ocean water

In 1914 as now, Tahoe City, on Lake Tahoe's shores, was a quiet family resort in marked contrast to the neon extravagances that would spring up around casinos on the Nevada side of the lake.

is tepid, beaches are plentiful and languorous, and the waves are perfect for surfing. The Central Coast is a wild, rocky place with steep mountains to one side, sheer cliffs to the other, and rocks jutting through the crashing surf. Blankets of fog and mist often anoint the shoreline of the state's northern rain forest. The entire coast is a wildlife-watcher's delight. Pelicans, herons, crabs, sea lions, two varieties of seals, and a half-dozen kinds of whales frolic there in plain sight.

The southernmost point on the coast, San Diego, is a beauteous place to begin an exploration of the immense Golden State. San Diego County stretches from the Mexican border at Tijuana to the U.S. Marines' training base at Camp Pendleton, and eastward from the ocean to the fringes of the Anza-Borrego Desert. But it is surprisingly mountainous, too; California Institute of Technology's acclaimed Palomar Observatory looms high in the Cleveland National Forest in the northern part of the county. Balmy San Diego has some of California's premier man-made marvels, from its world-class zoo and stunning collection of yachts at harbor to three old Spanish missions and the grand Del Coronado resort hotel to the festive plaza at Old Town State Historic Park and a re-created Victorian neighborhood at Heritage Park. A must-see is Balboa Park, named for the Spanish explorer who first spotted the Pacific Ocean in 1513.

To the east of San Diego and south of the man-made Salton Sea in the vast Imperial Valley lies an astonishing agricultural tableau. The lands around bustling El Centro are green with onions, spinach, sugar beets, and a dozen other crops that flourish year-round in what, without the trickling waters from the All-American Canal, would be arid no man's land. This is low country. Each Christmastide, the little town of Calipatria, near El Centro, strings holiday lights up its 184-foot municipal flagpole. The star at the top is at sea level.

The nearby Mojave desert is largely parched and unirrigated. Thermometer readings of

125 degrees Fahrenheit are not unusual in Death Valley or the scrubby sands near Needles. The U.S. record of 134 degrees was measured at Death Valley's Greenland Ranch, 178 feet below sea level, in 1913. Yet every season save summertime in the desert is so tolerable, visitors by the hundreds of thousands come to play golf, ride or surf the dunes, or hike amid the stark surroundings. Spindly Joshua trees cluster in a national park near the town of Twentynine Palms, blinding-white salt beds line several valley floors, and minerals turn patches of wasteland bright orange or yellow.

Death Valley is just sixty miles south of soaring Mount Whitney. There are desert oases, including the golf, tennis, and Hollywood star retreat of Palm Springs. There is even a luxury resort, the Furnace Creek Inn—complete with lush gardens, natural springs, and an azure swimming pool—in the heart of forbidding Death Valley. Gateway to the entire California desert—and to Las Vegas a state away—is Barstow, once a small railroad town and now a progressive city that features both historical attractions (including the state's most famous restored ghost town at Calico) and modern ones (120 name-brand outlet stores). The Calico Early Man "dig," one of the most important archaeological sites in North America, is fifteen miles from town, and some of the world's best-preserved insect and animal fossils—including that of a giant dog-bear creature—can be seen in Rainbow Basin, also nearby.

Orange County, sandwiched between San Diego and Los Angeles, might well have been written off by visitors as a humdrum bedroom community had not Walt Disney selected seventy-five acres amid an Anaheim citrus grove to build Disneyland, his first amusement park, in 1955. Combined with the rides and ghost town of nearby Knott's Berry Farm, which preceded it, and the lure of the county's Newport, Huntington, and Laguna beaches, Disneyland transformed Orange County into the sizzling tourist destination it remains today.

Los Angeles County was once maligned around the state as the "Queen of the Cow Counties." Grazing cattle and lemon groves once marked the landscape where today sprawling Los Angeles—with seventy independent cities in the county—and towns like Riverside in adjacent jurisdictions spread a blanket of twinkling lights halfway to Arizona. (Just ask anyone who has

One of the greatest Depression-era construction projects was the Shasta Dam, which is 602 feet high with a spillway three times higher than Niagara Falls. The dam provides water and cheap electricity to the lush Central Valley.

flown over the Southland at night.) Some of those lights belong to Hollywood dream factories—great movie studios that are now spread across chaparral canyons and elegant neighborhoods throughout the city. "L.A." also means the marble floors and overstuffed leather chairs of renovated Union train station, the swank Polo Lounge inside the "Pink Palace" Beverly Hills Hotel, vibrant shops along old Olvera Street, jazz under the stars at Hollywood Bowl, a Ferris Wheel ride at Santa Monica Pier, an elegant trip through history inside the Queen Mary at Long Beach, and a chance to commune with great art at the J. Paul Getty Museum on the billion-dollar, 110-acre Getty Center cultural campus in the Brentwood Hills.

Even though Route 66 carried millions of newcomers to Southern California through the eastern counties of Riverside and San Bernardino, the post-World War II boom seemed to bypass them. So in the 1950s Riverside and San Bernardino took to calling themselves the "Inland Empire." The campaign caught on, freeways reached the area, and Californians and out-of-state visitors alike began to appreciate the orange groves, ski resorts, art museums, botanical gardens,

rich forestland, and hot-air ballooning centers in this middle ground between Palm Springs and Los Angeles. In places with exotic names like Temecula, Hesperia, Blue Jay, and Rancho Cucamonga, one can pick apples, browse for antiques, slither down the world's tallest water slide, take a jeep tour, catch a light opera, or even see a stuffed television hero—Trigger, the horse pal of singing cowboy Roy Rogers.

California's Central Coast, stretching from Ventura and Santa Barbara north past Monterey Bay, calls itself the "Middle Kingdom." It is a place of staggering beauty and unlimited charm as Highway One winds past historic lighthouses, craggy oceanside cliffs, working wharves, and a half-dozen historic missions. Sun-drenched cities like Santa Barbara and San Luis Obispo are Mediterranean-style masterpieces where life seems like an ongoing festival. Deep valleys and rocky bays carve the coastline. At Pismo Beach—famous for the "Pismo clam," thousands of which were once harvested each day in the shallow waters—visitors may still drive their automobiles onto the compacted sand and scoop up a very limited number of clams.

Northward, the coastline turns wild. "It's nearly impossible to get to California's violently inhospitable Big Sur coast," wrote the *Washington Post* in 1998. "That's why everybody wants to." The newspaper quoted author Henry Miller, who was awed by his visit: "If the soul were to choose an arena in which to stage its agonies this would be the place for it. One feels exposed—not only to the elements, but to the sight of God." Big Sur got its name from Spaniards living in Monterey, who called the rugged coastline *El Sur Grande*—"the Big South." Here, the Santa Lucia Mountains rise vertically above the sea. There's only one road, the zigzagging, precarious, two-lane Highway One. Locals called Bixby Bridge, over Rocky Creek, "Rainbow Bridge" for the shape of the 320-foot arch below its span. This was an engineering marvel when it was built in 1932, but, as Tomi Kay Lussier points out in her *Complete History & Guide* to Big Sur, "its $250,000 construction cost wouldn't even purchase a small cabin in these hills" today.

The Mad River Railroad—affectionately known locally as the "Annie and Mary Train" in honor of women at each end of the short line—brought redwood logs from Blue Lake (here) to Arcata on the coast.

Nor would it buy much of a homestead on the cultured Monterey Peninsula. There, a collection of small cities like Monterey, Pacific Grove, and Seaside define the good life in this old Spanish provincial capital. The climate is agreeable; the wines, restaurant fare, and museums exquisite; the sunsets over the sapphire Monterey Bay mesmerizing. There are more than sixty fine art galleries in Carmel-by-the-Sea alone. Even the sea lions, crowding onto rocky outcroppings off the scenic, private, but tourable (for a fee) "17-Mile Drive" can't help but take it easy here.

California is often described as two irreconcilable entities, north and south. Indeed in 1859, nine years after statehood, the legislature voted to split the elongated state in two. The measure died only because Congress, nervous about creating new states as the drumbeat for civil war grew louder, ignored the idea.

Like the Southland, Northern California has its urban sprawl. It is the Bay Area, stretching from San Francisco southward through the Silicon Valley to Palo Alto and San Jose, and back up the west side of the Bay through Hayward to Oakland and Berkeley. There is no need to search for a core city here. Sophisticated San Francisco *is* "the City" for the whole region. There's but one freeway in the City by the Bay. People *walk*, even up and down the city's forty-three steep, identifiable hills. Public transit, including the beloved cable cars, has been entrenched for a century. A symphony hall, opera house, world-class art museums, theaters, rows of "painted lady" Victorian houses, two of the world's most photographed bridges, and the street that ushered in the "Summer of Love" in the 1960s are short taxi rides apart. However, you will need a ferry to reach another attraction: brooding Alcatraz Prison on an island in the middle of San Francisco Bay.

Grapevines were introduced to the ranchos surrounding Northern California missions by Franciscan friars in the 1770s. Later, more than three hundred varieties of European grapes—from chardonnay to pinot noir—thrived in the sandy soil of the Napa and Sonoma valleys north of San Francisco. Wine has become an important export of the Central Coast, from Santa Barbara to the Monterey Peninsula, as well. California introduced the deep-red and fruity Zinfandel, the only California grape varietal grown exclusively in the United States. Despite the advent of boutique winemaking in a score of other states, California's more than four hundred wineries still dominate the U.S. wine market. There is even a brandy distillery in the Napa Valley. Awaken at a hacienda-style inn in California's Wine Country, look out upon the sunswept hillsides planted in arrow-straight rows of vines, and you will swear you were in Greece or the south of France. But those areas do not offer an Old Faithful geyser as Calistoga, California, does. Or a petrified forest (also near Calistoga), gourmet dining and wine-tasting aboard a "wine train" (departing from Napa), or a late-winter Mustard Festival (celebrated throughout the Napa Valley).

California's northernmost counties are heavily forested, save for the northeast corner where oddities like lava tubes dot the otherworldly landscape of Lava Beds National Monument on the Modoc Plateau. The coastline of Mendocino County in the Sinkyone Wilderness is so unspoiled it is called the "Lost Coast." Aside from quaint fishing centers like Eureka, abundant freshwater lakes, and the majestic Cascade Range, extreme Northern California is marked by boundless stretches of green ponderosa pines, Douglas fir, spruce, giant sequoias, redwoods,

Even before it was wine country, California's Napa Valley was famous for its healing waters. From the 1870s to the 1920s, San Francisco's well-to-do sought rejuvenation at Napa Soda Springs resort.

San Francisco's devastating 1906 earthquake virtually demolished the eastern half of the city, including China-town. The quake itself did modest damage; fires that ignited ruptured gas lines destroyed downtown and many great mansions.

cedars, and hemlocks. Some of the redwood and sequoia trees are not just tall, they are colossal. Cars look like toys passing beside—or through!—some of the giant redwoods, many of which have been dated to A.D. 500 or earlier.

The California Northland does not lack for rain or snow. Forty inches of precipitation a year are normal, compared with zero to ten inches in the deserts of Inyo, San Bernardino, and Imperial counties to the south. (Zero inches is not an exaggeration; meteorologists have recorded no measurable precipitation for up to *two years* running in some California desert locations.) The dominant landmark is massive, usually snow-capped, volcanic Mount Shasta, and the region abounds in ghost towns, historical museums, and Victorian homes—seventy-five in little Yreka alone. In Fort Ross, an old church from the days of Russian settlement still stands. Near Fort Bragg, on the Mendocino Coast, visitors who ride the California Western Railroad's historic "Skunk Trains" need not jangle along in a vintage coach; they can opt to join the engineer in the open cab of the train's diesel engine or Baldwin steam locomotive.

Gold Country, reaching southward in a narrow band of the Sierra foothills below Sacramento, features bleak old Folsom Prison, still operating next to a modern penal institution; the Nevada Theater, the state's oldest continuously operating theater (where Mark Twain lectured) in Nevada City; and Columbia State Historical Park, California's best-preserved gold-mining town, where gold panning, stagecoach rides, and sips of sarsaparilla are still the order of the day. Panning skills could come in handy, for geologists speculate that 70 percent of California's gold has yet to be discovered. The Old Sacramento section of the state capital holds the largest concentration of restored buildings in the West and the largest railroad museum in North America—fitting for the city where the first transcontinental trains began their journey east.

This is San Francisco's ornate Palace Hotel at the time of its reopening following the Great Quake of '06. The hotel survived the earthquake only to burn to the ground when firefighters drained its private reservoir.

There is a monument, too, to the Pony Express, which terminated in Sacramento as well, and an elegant paddle-wheel steamer along the waterfront.

California's sublime Central Valley is one of the largest valleys in the world. If the entire Appalachian Mountain chain could somehow be lifted and moved west, it could be plopped into this valley. This is incredibly rich farmland thanks to its temperate year-round climate, moderate rainfall, and abundant water diverted from the rivers that wend down the Sierras' western slopes. Twenty-five percent of America's table food originates here, and the three leading U.S. counties in value of agricultural products sold, according to the 1992 Census of Agriculture, were Fresno, Tulare, and Kern—all in this valley. Wildlife refuges that protect migratory birds here are magnets for birders. But perhaps the favorite visitor activity is sampling food from cheese to strawberries to—believe it or not—jalapeño-flavored pistachio nuts. Fresno, at the heart of it all, offers an amazing assortment of small museums and a sixty-two-mile self-guided, late-winter Blossom Trail tour of peach, plum, nectarine, and almond trees in full bloom.

"Give me men to match my mountains," reads an inscription in the state capitol. Just inland from the Pacific is the narrow Coastal Range, full of fault lines and passes. These are mostly modest mountains, but at least one peak in each of the San Gabriel, San Bernardino, and Santa Rosa ranges tops ten thousand feet. One of California's attractions is that even residents of the Los Angeles Basin can, on a clear day, see the peaks around Big Bear Lake, and the magnificent San Bernardino Range is only an hour or so beyond. Northern Californians take to the hills too, of course, but many more gravitate to the grassy hills and quiet beaches of Golden Gate National Recreation Area, the wild expanse of Point Reyes National Seashore, or any number of magnificent city parks from Redding to San Jose.

Across the state to the east is the taller, far more precipitous Sierra Nevada Range, California's granite backbone. The Sierras reach from volcanic Mount Shasta in Siskiyou County in the green woods, six hundred miles south to Mount San Jacinto in Riverside County, overlooking the high desert. The Sierras are laced with picturesque lakes, trout streams, whitewater rapids beckoning to rafters, and natural trails. Here, as arriving settlers learned to their peril, there are few passes. There are, however, steep gorges; one falls ten thousand feet in ten miles, down to Owens Lake. The Yosemite Valley's alpine meadows butt into glacial rock walls from which waterfalls cascade. Here, the earth's largest known chunk of granite, *El Capitan*, towers thirty-two hundred feet above Yosemite Valley. In two lesser-visited national parks, Sequoia and Kings Canyon, giant trees—hundreds of years old—rival those in the California Northland.

Anglers, houseboaters, and skiers flock to Lake Tahoe, 6,229 feet above sea level, where the surrounding peaks soar another four to five thousand feet above the lake. Lake Tahoe's depth averages one thousand feet, and if California could be flattened and Lake Tahoe's water spread across the entire state, residents and visitors would be perpetually sloshing through more than fourteen inches of water. The environs offer the greatest concentration of alpine and cross-country ski trails in North America. The lake itself is shared with the State of Nevada; gaudy casinos line the Nevada shoreline, while rustic "Tahoe style" cabins and condominiums are the lure in California communities like South Lake Tahoe, Tahoe City, and Tahoma. A North Lake Tahoe brochure boasts, "Sails are fuller, boulders are bolder, jumpers jump higher, rollerbladers roll smoother, deer are dearer, museums less musty, trails more dusty, special events are more special, families closer, worries farther."

William Randolph Hearst spared no expense building his retreat, which he called "Casa Grande," in the Santa Lucia Mountains sixteen hundred feet above San Simeon Bay. Begun in 1922, construction continued until 1947.

There is an informal "California style," a leisure mentality that has permeated every aspect of American life from "dress-down Fridays" at the stuffiest of corporate offices to nationwide fixations with gardening, fitness, and outdoor recreation. Whereas citizens inside the Washington, D.C., Beltway may often be found talking politics, Louisianians discoursing about food, New Yorkers comparing the merits of their sports teams, and Americans in the remaining states discussing their jobs or the weather, Californians love to extol their *avocations*. One may be an avid hiker, another an inveterate bicyclist or rollerblader, still another a passionate sailor or surfer or snorkler. It is no accident that, in this state of extremes, San Diego became the unofficial capital of "extreme sports" that do not require snow but *do* involve daredevilry of all descriptions. It is in the Golden State, too, that citizens and visitors can fill their idle hours at the Banana Slug Derby, the Poison Oak Festival, the Doo Dah Parade, an Outhouse Race, or at the Jumping Frog Jubilee, the last made famous by Mark Twain during his residence on "Jackass Hill" in Tuolomne County. California even publishes a guide to motorcycle touring.

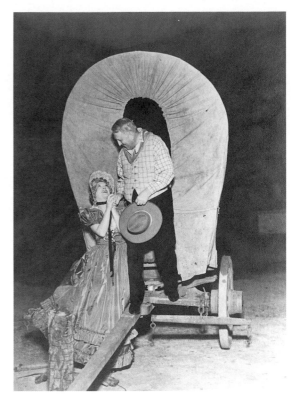

Hearst loved to throw costume parties at Hearst Castle for his Hollywood pals. Here, he and his mistress, Marion Davies, strike a frontier pose for one of the bashes.

There is an identifiable "California cuisine" that utilizes freshly harvested products which reflect the state's mix of cultures. Among the selections: cioppino, a fish stew combining Dungeness crab, littleneck clams, shrimp, tomatoes, bell peppers, and savory herbs; "hangtown fries," which are not potatoes but are omelets made with fried oysters and bacon; "tri-tip steak," a Central Coast favorite made with triangular pieces of grilled "bottom sirloin"; fish tacos of battered whitefish, shredded cabbage, fresh salsa, and lime juice wrapped in warm corn tortillas; date shakes, a frosty concoction of whipped ice cream, milk, and chopped dates; phó, the national dish of Vietnam, which is a spicy noodle soup eaten for breakfast; and bite-sized dim sum appetizer morsels brought tray after tray to the table at Bay Area Cantonese restaurants. No recipe is needed to enjoy four other California favorites: fragrant sourdough bread, sweet Dungeness crabs, creamy avocados, and succulent steamed or stuffed artichokes.

California routinely ranks as the nation's most-visited state, accounting for at least 10 percent of the domestic leisure travel market. But Californians themselves are the state's tourism mainstays, accounting for more than 80 percent of "person trips" within the state. Not surprisingly, Mexico is California's leading international market, but Japan is second; more than one million Japanese visit the state each year.

And why not? California's guests have more alluring attractions from which to choose than there are days in a decade. Dozens of theme parks, two presidential libraries (Nixon in Yorba Linda and Reagan in Simi Valley), a score of science centers, museums on everything from cartoons to Chinese immigration to the work of John Steinbeck, bustling ethnic enclaves, an array of national and state parks, snow-capped peaks, glittering city lights, shimmering desert vistas, beckoning beaches and boardwalks, deep and tall woods, and the glamorous film and television milieu are irresistible draws. How could you sum up such a savory stew? California is variegated, unpredictable, delightfully wild, and suave all at once. Radio and television comedian Fred Allen once remarked that "California's a wonderful place to live—if you happen to be an orange!" It is also a wonderful place to visit, no matter what you are.

OVERLEAF: The evocative mural on Wilcox Avenue in Hollywood, part of the citywide murals project, was commissioned by the lingerie shop around the corner. Note "E.T." calling home in the lobby.

The celebrities who have earned a star on the sidewalk of the Hollywood Walk of Fame range from second tier—and many now-obscure—personalities to mega film, television, and radio stars. When a great entertainer like Frank Sinatra dies, fans flock to leave a remembrance at the celebrity's spot on Hollywood Boulevard (above). The famous 450-foot-long, 45-foot-tall, never-quite-straight HOLLYWOOD sign (right) was erected in 1923 in the hills above town—not to tout the movie business, however, but to promote a new housing development. For twenty-six years, the sign, visible for miles on clear days, read "HOLLYWOOD-LAND." Vandals have occasionally played pranks with the sign, and one actress jumped to her death from the letter "H." The sign is therefore better protected today.

"Hollywood" has become a generic term for the Los Angeles movie and television industry. The film industry was born along Sunset Boulevard in Hollywood but today is scattered throughout the far-flung city. Big movie studios like Paramount (left) offer popular tours of their stage and back lot facilities, and Universal Studios has added spectacular shows and rides for visitors. Tickets to television shows that have live audiences are a hot tourist item. Sunset Boulevard is still busy today, but as a lively nightspot of restaurants, bars, boutique hotels, and nightclubs like the House of Blues (above), which was moved to Hollywood from Clarksdale, Mississippi.

Judging by the number of people who take bus tours of stars' homes and buy "maps of the stars" in Hollywood and Beverly Hills, America is as star-struck as it was in the golden age of movies. People even love to get a glimpse of stars' former *homes*, or homes once owned by stars now deceased, like Jayne Mansfield's onetime villa in Bel-Air (right). The hope is that a star will step out to get the newspaper or water the lawn. Stars' gravesites are a draw, too. Marilyn Monroe's vault (opposite) can be found—with some difficulty—in the tiny Westwood Village Memorial Park and Mortuary, hidden behind the Wilshire Boulevard business district. Burt Lancaster, Dean Martin, Donna Reed, Truman Capote, and Eva Gabor are also buried there.

Soaring palm trees form a canopy over fashionable Beverly Hills Drive (opposite). The independent city, which is home to Rodeo Drive, one of the world's poshest shopping strips, has been the community of choice of many entertainment executives and stars. Century City's "Avenue of the Stars" (above), now a high-rise complex of offices, restaurants, movie theaters, and stores, gets its name from the old 20th Century Fox backlot that once occupied the spot in central Los Angeles. The Griffith Observatory (overleaf), in Griffith Park above the fashionable Los Feliz neighborhood east of Hollywood, sometimes offers more stunning views of Los Angeles below than the stars above. On clear nights, its Zeiss telescope is open to the public. The observatory and park are named, not for noted movie producer D.W. Griffith, but for developer and mining magnate Griffith J. Griffith, who donated the land.

The thirty-five-thousand-year-old La Brea Tar Pits (above) were one of Los Angeles's earliest tourist attractions. Its gooey pitch was used by residents to coat their dusty roads, repair their boats, and patch their roofs. Now part of the city's George C. Page Museum of La Brea Discoveries, the facility displays models of mastodons and other creatures that became stuck in the mire, and some of the more than one million fossils of reptiles, birds, and mammals—including one woman—found there. By contrast, one of Los Angeles's newest attractions is the gleaming Getty Center (opposite), which combines a spectacular art museum, gardens, and five research institutes. Permanent collections and changing exhibitions in five pavilions are arranged around a courtyard. The complex is accessible only by a tram that is boarded at the foot of the hillside site off the San Diego Freeway above Westwood.

Malibu (opposite) is the jewel of the Los Angeles seashore. Its views of the Pacific Ocean are prized by well-to-do homeowners including several movie and television stars. The hillsides have shown a nasty tendency to slide down to Highway One in the region's prolonged winter rainstorms, however. The waters off Malibu State Beach are regarded as among the nation's best for surfing and scuba-diving. Like Malibu, Venice has a lovely beach that is one of the raciest and most eclectic in California, but it is the canals (top left)—reminiscent of the community's Italian namesake—that set it apart. Marina del Rey (bottom left) is one of the world's largest, and most exclusive, yacht harbors. The vessel in the foreground is decked out for a wedding.

The restored 1874 Point Fermin Lighthouse (above) in San Pedro is now home to the harbor's park superintendent. The Point Vicente Light (right) was built in 1926 near what is now Rancho Palos Verdes to guide ships into San Pedro Harbor. It is famous for its light, however, not the one cast out to sea, but a mysterious, glowing apparition seen by the lighthouse's keepers and others that turned out to be a stray arc from its Fresnel lens refracted toward the ground, causing a "ghost." The Queen Mary (overleaf), berthed at Long Beach, was once the flagship of the Cunard White Star line. It is now a floating hotel and is open for nostalgic tours.

The Disney empire began at Disneyland (above) in Orange County in 1955. The park got a boost from Walt Disney's concurrent television series, which borrowed the Adventureland, Fantasy-land, Tomorrowland, and Frontierland themes that divided the amusement park. The creator of Mickey Mouse, Donald Duck, Goofy, and other beloved cartoon characters once lived in an apartment right on the park's "Main Street." Nearby Knott's Berry Farm is the nation's oldest theme park. Begun by Walter Knott in the 1920s as a Wild West-theme snack bar on his boysen-berry farm, the park added an Old Town (opposite) in the 1940s. Stagecoach rides, "shootouts," and gentle rides helped bring customers into Knott's famous "chicken dinner" restaurant. There, for a while, meals were served on Walter and Cordelia Knott's wedding china. Today, a high-tech rollercoaster has expanded the park's appeal. Jams and jellies are still popular souvenirs.

Robert Schuller's star-shaped Crystal Cathedral (opposite) in Garden Grove is a monument to the power of televangelism. The television preacher began his crusades in a drive-in theater. His weekly "Hour of Power" services now attract almost three thousand worshippers at the glass-and steel cathedral and millions of followers at home. Outside huge glass doors that open on Sunday mornings, those who prefer the comforts of their automobiles can still catch the services. Architect Philip Johnson designed the building, which features more than ten thousand panes of glass. In Yorba Linda, next to the Richard Nixon Library, Pat Nixon's beloved rose garden frames the late president's birthplace (above). Exhibits at the library recall Nixon's accomplishments as a world statesman but do not minimize the disgrace of his resignation. Visitors can even listen to Watergate tapes. The Nixons are buried in the garden.

California's most famous mission—the seventh of twenty-one along the El Camino Real from San Diego to Sonoma—is San Juan Capistrano (above). Swallows do come back to Capistrano each spring to roost at the mission. But despite the legend, they are not always punctual about arriving precisely on Saint Joseph's Day, March 19. Artists come, though, to paint the mission, which was almost ruined when Mexico secularized California's missions after winning its independence from Spain. At another landmark remembered in song, Santa Catalina Island (right) is a favorite weekend retreat just twenty-one miles offshore from Newport Beach. The cove at upscale La Jolla (overleaf) is a haven for strollers, snorkelers, scuba-divers, and shoppers. Art galleries and trendy restaurants are also magnets for tourism in this "Mediterranean" setting.

The Famous Chicken, arguably America's most famous sports mascot, lulls a cluster of sea lions to sleep with a bedtime story (opposite) on La Jolla Beach. Once popularly known as the "San Diego Chicken" because of his frequent appearances at Padre major-league baseball games, Ted Giannoulas never worked for the team. He got his start at a student radio station, volunteering to slip on the chicken outfit for an Easter giveaway promotion. Now he travels the world to delight crowds with his antics at sporting events, fairs, and conventions. Umpires, stuff-shirts, and vegetarians are not always amused. Real animals are the lure at San Diego's Sea World (above), the original in the company's chain of marine zoological parks. Performing whales and dolphins are the stars at the park on Mission Bay, but Sea World also takes in injured and abandoned aquatic animals.

San Diego (left) is America's sixth-largest city and one of its most beautiful urban places. The agreeable climate—almost never too hot or too cold, and rarely rainy—has lured hundreds of thousands of retirees to this diverse city on the Mexican border. Cultural tourist attractions range from visits to the world-famous San Diego Zoo to an evening with the California Ballet Company. A statue to Juan Rodríguez Cabrillo (above), the mysterious Spanish discoverer of California in 1542, is the centerpiece of the Cabrillo National Monument site. Cabrillo's logs were lost, details of his death later on the voyage are unclear, and no one knows where he is buried.

The Hotel Del Coronado (above), a legendary Victorian resort across the bay from San Diego, has played host to fourteen presidents, hundreds of world leaders, and countless entertainment stars. The "Del" was built in 1888. "Hospitality House" (right) welcomes visitors to Balboa Park, which was established in 1868 but gained many of its ornate buildings when the park hosted the 1915 Panama-Pacific Exposition. San Diego's zoo, museum of art, and aerospace museum are on the grounds. Fog and low clouds often obscured the beacon from the 1855 Old Point Loma Lighthouse (overleaf), so in 1891 its function was replaced by a newer lighthouse at the bottom of the hill.

Onions (left) are a fraction of the bounty in the lush, irrigated Imperial Valley near El Centro. The value of crops grown in the beautiful valley—ranging from dates to honey to Bermuda grass seed—top one billion dollars annually. California's citrus industry thrives in Riverside County (above) where orange, grapefruit, and lemon groves form an incredible oasis on the edge of a vast desert. The state's power companies are increasingly relying upon wind power from arrays of turbines such as this one at Banning Pass (overleaf). To be effective, the fields of turbines must be placed in areas where the wind is almost constantly blowing. Optimists predict that as much as 20 percent of U.S. electrical power could be generated from the wind by 2020.

Palm Springs (above) is a mecca for accomplished golfers, tennis players, and sun-worshipers. They can count on sun all but eleven days a year on average. There are more than eight thousand known swimming pools in Palm Springs and surrounding towns. Twentynine Palms is the home of the Joshua Tree National Monument (right). The trees and other desert plants thrive during rare moist periods and, in the words of the National Park Service, "bide their time" during long droughts. The man-made Salton Sea (overleaf), whose surface is 227 feet below sea level, was created by mistake in 1905 when engineers attempted to divert Colorado River water into the Imperial Valley.

Near Barstow, the principal town of the desert, is the Calico Ghost Town (opposite) where Kenneth Best plays the part of "Monk," proprietor of a crude silver mine. This is not a re-creation. In the 1880s and 1890s it was a boomtown surrounded by more than five hundred working mines. After silver prices collapsed and the town was virtually deserted, it was purchased and saved by Knott's Berry Farm owner Walter Knott. In 1966, he donated Calico to San Bernardino County for use as a regional park. The Mojave Desert (above) near Needles often reports the hottest temperatures in the nation. Hence it is referred to as a "natural furnace." This photograph caught a rare springtime interlude when plants got enough moisture to burst into bloom.

The photographs on these two pages were taken in the same vicinity, in Death Valley National Park, which, at more than three thousand square miles, is the largest national park in the continental United States. One shows the bleak, aptly named Funeral Mountains (above), which epitomize the desolation of the barren landscape whose scorching desert floor and blinding-white salt flats lie 190 or more feet below sea level. The other reveals a lush oasis (opposite)—a spring-fed pond at the Furnace Creek Inn & Ranch Resort. Built in 1927, the inn has been restored to its 1930s appearance. Golfers flock here even in the blistering heat of summer because of the stark vistas and the unnerving experience of hitting a golf ball in the increased gravity below sea level. In the early years, a flock of sheep kept the course's grass "mowed."

Death Valley's sand dunes (opposite) rise eighty-five feet or more above the desert floor. They are home to kangaroo rats, lizards, coyotes, kit foxes, and sidewinder snakes. Death Valley is forbidding enough in the baking summer sun; adding swirling sand on windy days makes the place almost unendurable. The valley's famous "twenty mule teams" typically pulled three wagons (top left), two loaded with borax— a versatile mineral used in everything from soap to water softeners—and one filled with water for an arduous journey to the town of Mojave, 165 miles away. Most teams actually consisted of eighteen mules and two horses, which had greater pulling power. In a corner of Death Valley are old limestone kilns (bottom left) where silver miners made charcoal for use in their crude smelters.

FOODLAND MARKETS

On the road to Yosemite National Park near Fresno, Marie Bickford's unusual mosaic (above) salutes the workers whose efforts help make California's Central Valley the nation's most productive agricultural region. The imaginative mural was commissioned by the Fresno Jaycees and Foodland Markets. The Upper Falls (opposite) at Yosemite are one of many scenic wonders. Here swollen by spring snow melt, these cascades and the even-longer Lower Falls were a favorite subject of intrepid outdoor photographer Ansel Adams. First-time visitors to California are astounded to see alpine scenes like this view of the High Sierras from Sonora Pass (overleaf). This route is often closed, even in spring and fall, by snowdrifts. Peaks are especially breathtaking on the eastern slope of the Sierras, which were formed in a cataclysmic uplift three million years ago. The western slopes are less imposing and more heavily settled.

The small peak rising in the center of an array of mountains is the famous "Half Dome" (opposite), often used as the trademark of Yosemite National Park. It is thought that glacial ice floes sheared off about one fourth (not one half) of the rock formation. Up Jackass Hill in Tuolumne County is a reproduction—the chimney and fireplace are original—of the cabin (top left) where Mark Twain lived in 1864 and 1865. Twain moved to California from Missouri in hopes of striking it rich in the mines, but he soon turned to writing. Jackass Hill was once a stopping place for packers carrying supplies to the Sierra gold and silver mines. The mountains are a ways off from a barn (bottom left) in the foothills near Sonora.

A livery stable (above) is one relic at Columbia State Historic Park in the heart of Sierra gold country. Today, Columbia is the best-preserved boomtown in the region that produced the famous "Mother Lode" of the California Gold Rush. The park, which includes a restored saloon, jail, blacksmith shop, and general store, is a popular destination for school living-history programs and family gatherings. Programs such as a Victorian Easter parade, miner's Christmas pageant, and "poison oak show" are highlights of the park's calendar. Angels Camp (right) prepares its streets for the famous annual Calaveras County Jumping Frog contest and festival made famous in a Mark Twain story in which a miner rigs the event by feeding another contestant's frog a load of buckshot.

A wedding party poses on the steps of the California State Capitol (left) in Sacramento. Completed in 1874, the Renaissance Revival-style building was extensively renovated in the 1970s. Old Folsom Prison (above) in the Sacramento suburbs was made famous by Johnny Cash in his song "Folsom Prison Blues." The prison is still in use next to a modern penal institution, but the town is far better known today as the site of a gigantic outlet mall. The jewel of the Sierra Nevada Mountains is Lake Tahoe (overleaf), which straddles the California-Nevada border. On the California side it's a rustic family, fishing, and ski resort. Gaudy casinos light up the Nevada side.

Shasta Dam (above), near Redding, systematically releases water that supplies the bountiful fields and orchards of California's Central Valley. For a look at the building of the enormous dam, see page 15. Shasta Dam also supplies a man-made lake that is one of California's most popular recreational areas. One of the nation's largest fleet of houseboats meanders on the lake. Boat trips depart O'Brien, on the lake's eastern shore, for Shasta Caverns— limestone caves full of stalactites and stalagmites. Mount Shasta (right), an enormous, dormant 14,162-foot volcano, dominates the landscape of far-northern California. Usually snow-covered, it anchors the southern Cascade Mountains, which range northward to Mount Ranier in Washington. Unlike the higher Mount Whitney, over in the Sierras, Shasta is not lost in a parade of peaks; it can be seen clearly as far away as Crater Lake in southern Oregon.

Along California's northern coast lies the world-famous Redwood Empire (opposite). Visitors who meander down the narrow, winding, thirty-three-mile Avenue of the Giants are dwarfed by old-growth trees that can reach 350 or more feet and live two thousand years. One monster—and irresistible stop for photographs—along the scenic road is even labeled the "Immortal Tree." The journey recaptures a simpler time when kitschy little family attractions like a huge room inside a redwood tree—not glitzy theme parks—were the tourism rage. One of those enduring photo ops is the Shrine Drive-Thru Tree (above). Legend, slowly fading, has it that this is the turf of the shaggy, elusive anthropoid "Bigfoot." Logging almost destroyed the redwood forest, but preservationist campaigns and the creation of both state and national redwood parks saved many groves of the fast-growing trees.

South of Eureka is Ferndale, a remarkable Victorian town and an old dairying center where downtown businesses and private homes like the Gingerbread Mansion (right) have been restored to elegance. Once a physician's home, the house was converted into Ferndale's general hospital in the 1920s. It has also served as the American Legion hall and an apartment building. It is now a cozy bed-and-breakfast inn complete with a colorful English garden. Ferndale was settled by immigrants from many European countries, and annual events like the Portuguese Holy Ghost Celebration are still held. Eureka's Carson Mansion (opposite) was built about 1884 by lumberman William Carson. Primarily made of redwood, the house makes use of exotic materials like white mahogany and onyx. It is now a private club.

You might think the wind machine at the Peju Province Winery (opposite) in Napa County's wine country was used to cool the delicate grape leaves and blossoms. Quite the contrary. It circulates the air on extremely chilly winter nights, hopefully keeping the plants from freezing. The Domaine Carneros winery (top left) in northern Napa Valley makes sparkling wines. The château was inspired by the Château de la Marquetterie in Champagne, France. Napa and Sonoma's legendary vineyard rows (bottom left) march up and down hillsides in near-perfect precision. The picturesque area loves any excuse to celebrate with food and wine. Napa's Mustard Festival each fall, for instance, lasts four days and features cabernet sauvignon on Sunday, chardonnay on Monday, merlot and pinot noir on Tuesday, and sparkling wine on Wednesday.

The Sea Ranch resort (above) on California Highway One along the remote Sonoma County coast—where Russian fur traders and Canadian and Mexican whiskey smugglers once operated—is a favorite getaway spot for people from the San Francisco Bay area. Sausalito (right) in Marin County is also a place where Bay-area resi-dents "get away from it all." Just up from the harbor are numerous art galleries, coffee shops, and boutiques. The North Coast's link to San Francisco is the Golden Gate Bridge (overleaf). Ninety years before the bridge was built in the 1930s, Captain John C. Frémont called the passage into San Francisco Bay the "Golden Gate."

The San Francisco–
Oakland Bay Bridge
forms a backdrop for
the street lamps of
San Francisco's
Embarcadero (left),
which runs from the
edge of the downtown
financial district past
the bustling ferry
terminal, tugboat and
cruise-ship berths to
Fisherman's Wharf.
Residents successfully
blocked plans to cover
the Embarcadero—
and block the view
of the Bay—with a
freeway. Indeed, only
short stretches of
freeway intrude into
the City by the Bay.
On bustling Market
Street, an information
kiosk doubles as a
newsstand (above).
Downtown has
gradually expanded
south of Market from
its tight quarters
above that busy artery.
"SoMa" (South of
Market) growth was
spurred by develop-
ment of the Moscone
Convention Center.

Beach Blanket Babylon, *at Club Fugazi, is the nation's longest-running revue and a wildly popular local and tourist attraction in San Francisco. It is loosely—very loosely—based on the story of Cinderella's search for her prince. One of the show's delights is an outrageous series of sight gags: oversized hats like the one worn by chanteuse Val Diamond (above). A now-familiar signature shot of San Francisco (right) is taken from Alamo Square. It shows the old—a series of "painted lady" Victorian houses—and the new—the modern downtown skyline. Most painted ladies have been subdivided into apartment units in San Francisco's tight housing market.*

Native Americans working for Franciscan friars completed San Francisco's Mission Dolores (opposite) in 1791, the oldest-standing building in San Francisco. The surrounding Mission District is the city's Hispanic hub renowned for its colorful murals. The cable car (top left) is not just a tourist attraction. San Franciscans ride the quaint cars, all pulled by moving cables just beneath the pavement. When horse-drawn carriages, and even early automobiles, could not negotiate the city's steep hills, cable cars zipped up and over them with ease. The principle is simple: they lock onto the cable to go, release from the cable to stop. Refurbished conventional trolleys (bottom left), most brought in from other cities, run out Market Street to the Castro, San Francisco's largely gay and lesbian quarter.

101

Haight-Ashbury (above), the vortex of the "tune in, turn on, drop out" generation of the 1960s, clings to some of its counter-culture mystique. The neighborhood is now seedy in spots, gentrified in others, and it is tightly patrolled by San Francisco police. Still, tour buses cruise Haight Street so visitors can check out the "freaks." San Francisco's colorful Chinatown (right), the largest Chinese population outside of Asia, is full of herbal pharmacies, curio shops, hundreds of restaurants and dim-sum parlors, and exotic markets. It is still largely confined to the forty-two-square block area that was virtually destroyed by the terrible 1906 earthquake, then rebuilt. The unofficial death toll in the Great Quake was one thousand citywide, but hundreds more undocumented Chinese likely perished.

Coit Tower (opposite) atop Telegraph Hill was a gift from Lillie Coit who had been saved from a conflagration by a fire company as a girl. She married well and bequeathed funds to build a memorial to firefighters. Some say it is more than a coincidence that the tower resembles the nozzle of a fire hose. Frank Heaney (left) was once the youngest correctional officer at Alcatraz, the hard-time penitentiary in San Francisco Bay that was reserved for the federal system's "worst of the worst" offenders, a list that included Al Capone, George "Machine Gun" Kelly, and Robert Stroud— the "Birdman of Alcatraz." The Palace of Fine Arts (overleaf) is a permanent 1960s re-creation of the temporary Beaux-Arts buildings used for San Francisco's version of the 1915 celebration of the opening of the Panama Canal.

Filoli (above) in Woodside, near Palo Alto, is a 654-acre estate—world famous for its gardens—now owned by the National Trust for Historic Preservation. The name came from the first two letters of three words: Fight, Love, and Live. They come from a credo that the estate's builder, William Bowers Bourne II, admired: "Fight for a just cause, love your fellow man, live a good life." The 1903 Memorial Church (right) is the focal point of Stanford University, which was endowed by Leland Stanford, one of the state's "Big Four" railroad tycoons. The chapel and adjacent buildings are meant to suggest a mission complex. Pigeon Point Lighthouse (overleaf), on Highway One between San Francisco and Monterey Bay, is now a hostel.

Monterey is usually busy and often festive as on this market day (left). The town was the Spanish, and then Mexican, capital of California. Author Robert Louis Stevenson lived in this Monterey house (above) as he soaked up atmosphere and found inspiration for his classic novel Treasure Island. *The oldest part of the house dates to 1840. Stevenson boarded there in 1879 while courting his future wife, Fanny Osborne. Now part of a state museum complex, the house features Stevenson's furniture and memorabilia. Stevenson also wrote about the wild Big Sur coastline, calling it "the greatest meeting of land and sea in the world."*

Once the world's
sardine capital,
Monterey is still a
busy fishing port
(opposite). Cannery
Row, immortalized by
writer John Steinbeck,

is now a gallery of
shops, restaurants,
motels, and one of
the nation's great
aquariums. Colorful
restaurants and
fishmonger stands

thrive amid the
fishing operations on
the pier as well. The
old Custom House
(above) was the
center of commerce
when Monterey was

Mexico's only point
of entry on the Alta
California coast.
Ship captains bound
for any port from
San Diego to San
Francisco were sup-

posed to register—
and pay duties on—
their cargoes.
Many ignored the
requirement and
never dropped
anchor in Monterey.

This figure (above) is a touchstone of the Hog's Breath restaurant and bar in Carmel-by-the-Sea owned by actor—and former mayor—Clint Eastwood. Missionary priest Junipero Serra, who also founded eight other missions in California, lived and died in the Carmel Mission Basilica (right). In the late 1700s, when crops were abundant, the Native American population there numbered around one thousand. European diseases steadily reduced that population. In 1987, Pope John Paul II visited Carmel mission during his tour of the United States. The French Country-style Château Julien Winery (overleaf) in the beautiful Carmel Valley has been producing Johannisberg Rieslings, cream sherries, chardonnays, and other varieties since 1982.

The drive along Highway One near Big Sur (left) is breathtaking. Civilization rarely intrudes. Spanish colonists at Carmel called the area to the south of their town "big country." The Little Sur River empties into the sea there (above). Farther down the coast, on a mountaintop above the village of San Simeon, visitors walk through newspaper baron William Randolph Hearst's "castle" with wonderment. The publisher's Hollywood friends often joined him and his mistress, Marion Davies, for a dip in the incredible Neptune Pool (overleaf). Hearst imported authentic ancient columns and friezes for the 104-foot-long white marble pool. A Parisian sculptor was brought in to create the surrounding statues.

A celery crop (above) stretches far into the distance in a field near Los Almos on the Central Coast. Soaker hoses laid down the middle of each row keep the tender plants watered. Near Cambria, also on that coast near San Simeon, wildflowers (right) grow in abundance on the bluffs. The purple flower is lupine. This array is found on the private East-West Ranch; the owners have generously opened their property to walkers. Elsewhere in the area, flowers are widely grown for their seeds, which are then shipped by mailorder houses around the world. The blooms are then sold, at cut-rate prices, locally. Mercury was once mined in the hills near Cambria, but the area is now a haven for artists.

Relaxing Santa Barbara is one of the most architecturally consistent spots in all of California. Red tile roofs abound on mission-style buildings throughout the city. State Street and the courtyards that lead from it (opposite) are festive places jammed with shoppers and browsers on weekends. The city is loaded with street cafés, small pubs, and sushi bars. Even the city's university has a "laid-back" reputation within the state's higher educational system. Mission Santa Barbara itself (above) was founded by the Franciscans as a base from which to convert the population of Santa Barbara Indians. El Camino Real bells were placed near each of the state's missions along U.S. Highway 101. Some have even withstood the depredations of vandals.

Index

This whimsical tree-house is one of the attractions found along the thirty-three-mile Avenue of the Giants in California's redwood country. The gargantuan trees have been turned into all sorts of tourist draws, but the mighty trees are attractions enough themselves. While kids cavort among the curiosities, adults can get a thorough understanding of the area's natural history at the visitor center.